Vegan Type-2 Diabetic Die

VEGAN TYPE 2 DIET COOKBOOK FOR NEWLY DIAGNOSED

Nourish Plant-Based Recipes with Low Carbohydrates for Pre-diabetes Management and Type-2 Diabetes Reversal, Accompanied by a 4-Week Meal Plan.

Emily O. Wells

Copyright © 2024 by *Emily O. Wells*

All rights reserved. No part of this publication may be reproduced, distributed, or transmitted in any form or by any means, including photocopying, recording, or other electronic or mechanical methods, without the prior written permission of the publisher, except in the case of brief quotations embodied in critical reviews and certain other noncommercial uses permitted by copyright law.

Disclaimer

This book is intended to provide educational information on the topic of managing type-2 diabetes through a plant-based diet.

However, the author and publisher are not responsible for any consequences arising from the use of information contained in this book. Readers are advised to consult with their healthcare provider before making any significant dietary or lifestyle changes, especially if they have pre-existing medical conditions or concerns.

INTRODUCTION

As the sun dipped below the horizon, casting a warm glow over the kitchen, I watched my mother, her brow furrowed in concentration, flipping through the pages of the Vegan Type 2 Diabetic Diet Cookbook. For years, she had battled with the relentless grip of type 2 diabetes, navigating through a path of medications and dietary restrictions.

With determination etched across her face, she embarked on a journey fueled by the knowledge gathered within these pages. Gone were the days of flavorless, uninspired meals; instead, our kitchen became a sanctuary of creativity and nourishment. We chopped vibrant vegetables, simmered fragrant spices, and **explored the endless possibilities of plant-based cooking.**

Weeks turned into months, and with each passing day, I witnessed a remarkable transformation in my mother. Her energy levels soared, her blood sugar levels stabilized, and a newfound vitality radiated from within. As she savored each delicious bite, I could see the joy dancing in her eyes, a testament to the power of wholesome, plant-based nutrition.

With the guidance of this cookbook, she reclaimed control over her health, one delectable meal at a time. And as we shared laughter and love around the dinner table, I knew that together, we had rewritten the narrative of her journey with type 2 diabetes.

Vegan Type-2 Diabetic Diet Cookbook | 2024

CHAPTER 1 — 12

UNDERSTANDING TYPE 2 DIABETES — 12

Overview of Type 2 Diabetes: — 12

Causes and Risk Factors: — 13

Importance of Diet in Managing Type 2 Diabetes: — 13

Benefits of a Plant-Based Diet: — 14

THE BASICS OF A VEGAN TYPE 2 DIABETIC DIETS — 18

What is a Vegan Diet? — 18

Guidelines for a Vegan Type 2 Diabetic Diets — 18

Nutritional Considerations — 19

Tips for Transitioning to a Vegan Lifestyle — 21

PLANNING YOUR MEALS: THE IMPORTANCE OF MEAL PLANNING — 23

How to Create a Balanced Meal Plan: — 25

Tips for Successful Meal Prep: — 26

VEGAN TYPE 2 DIABETIC BREAKFAST RECIPES: — 28
1. Berry Chia Overnight Oats — 29
2. Avocado Toast with Tomato — 30
3. Tofu Scramble with Spinach and Mushrooms — 31
4. Fruit and Nut Granola Bar — 32

5. Green Smoothie	33
6. Whole Grain Cereal with Fruit	33
7. Almond Butter Banana Toast	34
8. Spinach and Mushroom Breakfast Wrap	35
9. Quinoa Breakfast Bowl	36
10. Blueberry Oat Pancakes	36

VEGAN TYPE 2 DIABETIC LUNCH RECIPES — 38

1. Quinoa Salad with Roasted Vegetables	38
2. Chickpea and Vegetable Stir-Fry	39
3. Lentil and Vegetable Soup	40
4. Tofu and Vegetable Stir-Fry	41
5. Black Bean and Sweet Potato Burrito Bowl	42
6. Mediterranean Chickpea Salad	43
7. Tofu Veggie Wrap	44
8. Roasted Vegetable and Hummus Sandwich	45
9. Spinach and Mushroom Vegan Frittata	46
10. Stuffed Bell Peppers with Quinoa and Black Beans	47

VEGANS TYPE 2 DIABETIC DINNER RECIPES: — 49

1. Quinoa-Stuffed Bell Peppers	49
2. Lentil Vegetable Soup	50
3. Chickpea and Vegetable Stir-Fry	51
4. Spaghetti Squash with Marinara Sauce	52
5. Tofu and Vegetable Stir-Fry with Brown Rice	54
6. Mushroom and Spinach Risotto	55
7. Veggie Burger with Sweet Potato Fries	56
8. Chickpea and Vegetable Curry	58
9. Vegan Chili with Beans and Lentils	59
10. Roasted Vegetable and Quinoa Salad	60

VEGANS TYPE 2 DIABETIC DINNER RECIPES: — 62

1. Quinoa-Stuffed Bell Peppers	62

2. Lentil Vegetable Soup	63
3. Chickpea and Vegetable Stir-Fry	64
4. Spaghetti Squash with Marinara Sauce	65
5. Tofu and Vegetable Stir-Fry with Brown Rice	67
6. Mushroom and Spinach Risotto	68
7. Veggie Burger with Sweet Potato Fries	69
8. Chickpea and Vegetable Curry	71
9. Vegan Chili with Beans and Lentils	72
10. Roasted Vegetable and Quinoa Salad	73

VEGANS TYPE 2 DIABETIC SNACK RECIPES: **75**

1. Chickpea Salad	75
2. Almond Butter Apple Slices	76
3. Edamame Hummus with Carrot Sticks	76
4. Roasted Chickpeas	77
5. Berry Chia Pudding	78
6. Vegetable Sushi Rolls	78
7. Greek Yogurt with Berries and Almonds	79
8. Spicy Roasted Cauliflower	80
9. Stuffed Mini Bell Peppers	81
10. Trail Mix	81

DESSERTS AND TREATS FOR TYPE 2 DIABETICS   **83**

1. Chia Seed Pudding	83
2. Baked Apples	84
3. Greek Yogurt Parfait	85
4. Dark Chocolate-Dipped Strawberries	86
5. Coconut Flour Banana Muffins	87
6. Avocado Chocolate Mousse	88
7. Cinnamon Baked Pears	89
8. Peanut Butter Banana Bites	90
9. Berry Yogurt Bark	91
10. Almond Flour Chocolate Chip Cookies	92

BEVERAGE OPTIONS SUITABLE FOR INDIVIDUALS WITH TYPE 2 DIABETES — 94

   1. Green Tea with Lemon: — 94
   2. Golden Milk: — 94
   3. Berry Smoothie: — 95
   4. Cucumber Mint Infused Water: — 95
   5. Coconut Water with Lime: — 97
   6. Iced Green Tea with Mint: — 97
   7. Almond Butter Protein Shake: — 97
   8. Hibiscus Iced Tea: — 98
   9. Sparkling Water with Citrus: — 98
   10. Ginger Turmeric Lemonade: — 100

4-WEEK MEAL PLAN FOR TYPE 2 DIABETES REVERSAL — 101

Week 1: Breakfast, Lunch, Dinner, and Snack Ideas — 101
  Day 1: — 101
  Day 2: — 101
  Day 3: — 102

Week 2: Meal Plan for Variety and Balanced Nutrition — 102
  Day 1: — 102
  Day 2: — 103
  Day 3: — 103

Week 3: Incorporating Different Flavors and Textures — 104
  Day 1: — 104
  Day 2: — 104
  Day 3: — 105

Week 4: Final Week of the Meal Plan with Suggested Modifications — 105
  Day 1: — 105

Day 2: 106
Day 3: 106
1. Fresh Produce: 107
2. Whole Grains: 107
3. Legumes: 108
4. Plant-Based Proteins: 108
5. Healthy Fats: 108
6. Dairy Alternatives: 109
7. Herbs, Spices, and Condiments: 109
8. Low-Glycemic Sweeteners: 109
9. Frozen Foods: 110
10. Miscellaneous: 110

GLOSSARY OF TERMS   **111**

CHAPTER 1

UNDERSTANDING TYPE 2 DIABETES

Type-2 diabetes is a metabolic disorder characterized by insulin resistance, where the body's cells become resistant to the effects of insulin, leading to elevated blood sugar levels. In this chapter, we will delve into the intricacies of type-2 diabetes, exploring its causes, risk factors, and the pivotal role of diet in its management. Additionally, we'll discuss the potential benefits of adopting a plant-based diet as a cornerstone of diabetes management and reversal.

Overview of Type 2 Diabetes:

Type 2 diabetes accounts for the majority of diabetes cases worldwide and is often associated with lifestyle factors such as poor diet, sedentary lifestyle, and obesity. Unlike type-1 diabetes, which is an autoimmune condition resulting in the destruction of insulin-producing cells in the pancreas; type 2 diabetes typically develops gradually and is characterized by insulin resistance and impaired insulin secretion.

Causes and Risk Factors:

Several factors contribute to the development of type 2 diabetes, including genetics, obesity, physical inactivity, poor diet, and age. Individuals with a family history of diabetes, those who are overweight or obese, and individuals with sedentary lifestyles are at increased risk. Additionally, certain ethnic groups, such as African Americans, Hispanics, and Native Americans, are more predisposed to developing type-2 diabetes.

Importance of Diet in Managing Type 2 Diabetes:

Diet plays a crucial role in the management of type 2 diabetes. By making mindful dietary choices, individuals can better control their blood sugar levels, improve insulin sensitivity, and reduce the risk of diabetes-related complications. A balanced diet that focuses on controlling carbohydrate intake, choosing healthy fats, and prioritizing whole, nutrient-rich foods is essential for managing type 2 diabetes effectively.

Benefits of a Plant-Based Diet:

Research suggests that adopting a plant-based diet may offer numerous benefits for individuals with type 2 diabetes. Plant-based diets are naturally low in saturated fats and cholesterol, making them conducive to heart health, a significant concern for people with diabetes who are at increased risk of cardiovascular disease. Additionally, plant-based diets are rich in fiber, vitamins, minerals, and phytonutrients, which can help improve insulin sensitivity, promote weight loss, and lower blood sugar levels.

Thus, the benefits of a plant-based diet are manifold, encompassing not only individual health but also environmental sustainability and animal welfare. Here's an extensive look at the various advantages:

1. Improved Heart Health: Plant-based diets are naturally low in saturated fats and cholesterol while being rich in heart-healthy nutrients like fiber, antioxidants, and unsaturated fats. Studies have consistently shown that adopting a plant-based diet can lower the risk of heart disease, hypertension, and stroke.

2. Weight Management: Plant-based diets tend to be lower in calories compared to diets rich in animal products. Additionally, the high fiber content of plant foods promotes satiety, reducing the likelihood of overeating. As a result, many individuals find it easier to achieve and maintain a healthy weight on a plant-based diet.

3. Better Blood Sugar Control: For individuals with type 2 diabetes or those at risk of developing the condition, a plant-based diet can be particularly beneficial. Whole plant foods are typically low on the glycemic index, meaning they cause smaller fluctuations in blood sugar levels. Additionally, the fiber and complex carbohydrates found in plant foods help regulate blood sugar levels and improve insulin sensitivity.

4. Lower Risk of Chronic Diseases: Numerous studies have linked plant-based diets to a reduced risk of chronic diseases such as cancer, diabetes, and neurodegenerative disorders. The abundance of vitamins, minerals, antioxidants, and phytochemicals found in plant foods help protect cells from damage, inhibit the growth of cancer cells, and support overall health and longevity.

5. Gut Health: Plant-based diets are rich in fiber, which serves as fuel for beneficial gut bacteria. A healthy gut micro biome is essential for digestion, nutrient absorption, immune function, and even mental health. By promoting a diverse and thriving micro biota, plant-based diets contribute to overall well-being.

6. Environmental Sustainability: Plant-based diets have a significantly lower environmental footprint compared to diets rich in animal products. The production of plant foods requires fewer natural resources such as land, water, and energy, and generates fewer greenhouse gas emissions. By choosing plant-based foods, individuals can help mitigate climate change and preserve ecosystems.

7. Animal Welfare: One of the ethical pillars of a plant-based diet is its emphasis on reducing harm to animals. By abstaining from meat, dairy, and other animal products, individuals can minimize their contribution to animal suffering in the food industry.

Chapter 2:

The Basics of a Vegan Type 2 Diabetic Diets

What is a Vegan Diet?

A vegan diet is centered on plant-based foods while excluding all animal products, including meat, dairy, eggs, and honey. Instead, it prioritizes fruits, vegetables, whole grains, legumes, nuts, seeds, and plant-based alternatives. By embracing a vegan diet, individuals not only improve their health but also contribute to environmental sustainability and animal welfare.

Guidelines for a Vegan Type 2 Diabetic Diets

Creating a balanced vegan type 2 diabetic diet involves mindful selection of nutrient-rich foods to support blood sugar control and overall health. Key guidelines include:

1. Emphasize Whole Foods: Base your meals around whole, minimally processed plant foods such as fruits, vegetables, whole grains, legumes, nuts, and seeds.

2. Control Carbohydrate Intake: Monitor portion sizes and choose complex carbohydrates with a low glycemic index to prevent blood sugar spikes. Incorporate plenty of fiber-rich foods to slow down digestion and promote satiety.

3. Prioritize Healthy Fats: Include sources of healthy fats such as avocados, nuts, seeds, and olive oil in moderation to support heart health and enhance nutrient absorption.

4. Monitor Protein Intake: Ensure an adequate intake of protein by including plant-based sources such as tofu, tempeh, legumes, nuts, seeds, and whole grains in your diet.

5. Limit Added Sugars: Minimize the consumption of processed foods, sugary beverages, and desserts to keep blood sugar levels stable.

Nutritional Considerations

In addition to macronutrients (carbohydrates, protein, and fat), individuals following a vegan type 2 diabetic diet must pay attention to certain micronutrients, including:

1. Vitamin B12: Consider supplementing with vitamin B12 or consuming fortified foods to prevent deficiency.

2. Calcium: Incorporate calcium-rich plant foods such as leafy greens, fortified plant milks, tofu, and almonds to support bone health.

3. Iron: Consume iron-rich plant foods such as lentils, beans, tofu, spinach, and quinoa, along with vitamin C-rich foods to enhance iron absorption.

4. Omega-3 Fatty Acids: Include plant-based sources of omega-3 fatty acids, such as flaxseeds, chia seeds, hemp seeds, walnuts, and algae-based supplements.

Tips for Transitioning to a Vegan Lifestyle

Transitioning to a vegan lifestyle can be a rewarding journey, but it may also present challenges, especially for individuals accustomed to omnivorous diets. Here are some practical tips to facilitate the transition:

1. **Start Gradually:** Experiment with incorporating more plant-based meals into your diet gradually, allowing your taste buds and digestion to adapt over time.

2. **Explore New Foods:** Embrace the diversity of plant-based foods by experimenting with unfamiliar ingredients and recipes. Get creative in the kitchen and explore different cuisines to keep meals exciting and enjoyable.

3. **Seek Support:** Connect with fellow vegans or join online communities for support, encouragement, and recipe inspiration. Consider consulting with a registered dietitian experienced in plant-based nutrition for personalized guidance.

4. **Focus on Variety:** Aim for a diverse array of plant foods to ensure you're meeting your nutritional needs and enjoying a well-rounded diet.

Chapter 3:

Planning Your Meals: The Importance of Meal Planning

The benefits of Meal Planning for Type 2 Diabetes are as follow:

1. **Blood Sugar Control:** Meal planning allows individuals to regulate their carbohydrate intake, choose foods with a low glycemic index, and maintain stable blood sugar levels throughout the day.

2. **Portion Control:** By pre-determining portion sizes and meal compositions, meal planning helps prevent overeating and ensures individuals consume appropriate amounts of nutrients without exceeding their energy needs.

3. **Nutritional Balance:** Planning meals in advance enables individuals to incorporate a variety of nutrient-dense foods into their diet, ensuring they meet their daily requirements for essential nutrients while minimizing the consumption of processed foods and empty calories.

4. **Time and Cost Efficiency:** Meal planning saves time and reduces the need for last-minute decisions about what to eat. It also facilitates budgeting and grocery shopping, as individuals can create shopping lists based on their planned meals, minimizing food waste and unnecessary expenses.

5. **Stress Reduction:** Having meals planned in advance reduces the stress and anxiety associated with mealtime decisions, especially for individuals managing busy schedules or juggling multiple responsibilities.

How to Create a Balanced Meal Plan:

1. Understand Dietary Guidelines: Familiarize yourself with dietary recommendations for individuals with type 2 diabetes, including guidelines for carbohydrate, protein, fat, and fiber intake.

2. Choose Nutrient-Dense Foods: Base your meals on whole, minimally processed foods such as fruits, vegetables, whole grains, legumes, lean proteins, and healthy fats.

3. Balance Macronutrients: Ensure each meal contains a balance of carbohydrates, protein, and healthy fats to promote satiety, stabilize blood sugar levels, and support overall health.

4. Consider Portion Sizes: Use portion control methods such as measuring cups, food scales, or visual cues to portion out appropriate servings of different food groups.

5. Incorporate Variety: Aim for variety in your meal plan by including a diverse range of foods from different food groups, colors, and textures to ensure you receive a wide array of nutrients.

Tips for Successful Meal Prep:

1. Set Aside Time: Dedicate a specific time each week for meal planning and preparation, allowing sufficient time to plan meals, create shopping lists, and cook in bulk if necessary.

2. Batch Cooking: Prepare large batches of staple foods such as grains, legumes, and proteins that can be incorporated into multiple meals throughout the week.

3. Use Storage Containers: Invest in quality storage containers to store prepped ingredients and cooked meals safely in the refrigerator or freezer.

4. Label and Date: Label containers with the name of the dish and the date it was prepared to ensure freshness and prevent food waste.

5. Stay Flexible: While it's essential to stick to your meal plan as much as possible, allow yourself flexibility to accommodate changes in schedule or preferences.

Chapter 4

VEGAN TYPE 2 DIABETIC BREAKFAST RECIPES:

I. **Nutrient-Dense Breakfast Ideas:** Start your day with nutrient-packed options like overnight oats with chia seeds and berries, avocado toast on whole grain bread with sliced tomatoes, or a tofu scramble with spinach and mushrooms.

II. **Quick and Easy Breakfast Recipes:** For busy mornings, whip up simple yet satisfying meals like whole grain toast with almond butter and banana slices, a bowl of whole grain cereal topped with plant-based milk and fresh fruit, or a fruit and nut granola bar for on-the-go convenience.

III. **Breakfast Smoothies and Juices:** Energize your morning with refreshing smoothies and juices made from a variety of fruits, leafy greens, and plant-based protein sources. Blend together ingredients like spinach, banana, almond milk, and protein powder for a green smoothie, or try juicing carrots, apples, and ginger for a vibrant morning pick-me-up.

However, herein are 10 Vegan Type 2 Diabetic Breakfast Recipes:

1. Berry Chia Overnight Oats

Ingredients:

- 1/2 cup rolled oats
- 1 cup almond milk
- 1 tablespoon chia seeds
- 1/2 cup mixed berries (fresh or frozen)
- 1 tablespoon chopped nuts (optional)

Instructions:

I. In a jar or bowl, mix oats, almond milk, and chia seeds.
II. Add mixed berries on top.
III. Cover and refrigerate overnight.
IV. In the morning, stir well and top with chopped nuts if desired.

Nutrient Value (per serving):

- Calories: 250
- Carbohydrates: 35g
- Protein: 7g

- Fat: 9g
- Fiber: 8g

2. Avocado Toast with Tomato

Ingredients:

- 2 slices whole grain bread
- 1 ripe avocado
- 1 tomato, sliced
- Salt and pepper to taste

Instructions:

I. Toast the bread slices until golden brown.
II. Mash the avocado and spread evenly onto the toast.
III. Top with sliced tomato.
IV. Season with salt and pepper to taste.

Nutrient Value (per serving):

- Calories: 280
- Carbohydrates: 27g
- Protein: 6g
- Fat: 18g
- Fiber: 9g

3. Tofu Scramble with Spinach and Mushrooms

Ingredients:

- 1/2 block firm tofu, crumbled
- 1 cup spinach
- 1/2 cup sliced mushrooms
- 1/4 teaspoon turmeric powder
- Salt and pepper to taste

Instructions:

I. In a non-stick skillet, sauté mushrooms until tender.
II. Add crumbled tofu and turmeric powder, and cook for 5 minutes.
III. Add spinach and cook until wilted.
IV. Season with salt and pepper to taste.

Nutrient Value (per serving):

- Calories: 180
- Carbohydrates: 7g
- Protein: 14g
- Fat: 10g
- Fiber: 3g

4. Fruit and Nut Granola Bar

Ingredients:

- 1 cup rolled oats
- 1/2 cup chopped nuts (almonds, walnuts, or pecans)
- 1/4 cup dried fruit (raisins, cranberries, or apricots)
- 1/4 cup maple syrup or agave nectar

Instructions:

I. Preheat oven to 350°F (175°C) and line a baking dish with parchment paper.
II. In a bowl, mix oats, chopped nuts, dried fruit, and maple syrup.
III. Press mixture evenly into the baking dish.
IV. Bake for 20-25 minutes or until golden brown.
V. Let cool, then cut into bars.

Nutrient Value (per serving):

- Calories: 200
- Carbohydrates: 26g
- Protein: 4g
- Fat: 9g
- Fiber: 3g

5. Green Smoothie

Ingredients:

- 1 cup spinach
- 1/2 cup frozen mixed berries
- 1/2 banana
- 1 tablespoon chia seeds
- 1 cup almond milk

Instructions:

I. Blend all ingredients until smooth.
II. Add more almond milk if needed to reach desired consistency.
III. Pour into a glass and enjoy immediately.

Nutrient Value (per serving):

- Calories: 200
- Carbohydrates: 25g
- Protein: 6g
- Fat: 9g
- Fiber: 9g

6. Whole Grain Cereal with Fruit

Ingredients:

- 1 cup whole grain cereal
- 1/2 cup sliced strawberries
- 1/4 cup blueberries
- 1 cup almond milk

Instructions:

I. Pour cereal into a bowl.
II. Top with sliced strawberries and blueberries.
III. Pour almond milk over the top and serve.

Nutrient Value (per serving):

- Calories: 250
- Carbohydrates: 45g
- Protein: 6g
- Fat: 5g
- Fiber: 8g

7. Almond Butter Banana Toast

Ingredients:

- 2 slices whole grain bread
- 2 tablespoons almond butter
- 1 banana, sliced

Instructions:

I. Toast the bread slices until golden brown.
II. Spread almond butter evenly onto each slice.
III. Top with sliced banana and serve.

Nutrient Value (per serving):

- Calories: 320
- Carbohydrates: 38g
- Protein: 8g
- Fat: 16g
- Fiber: 8g

8. Spinach and Mushroom Breakfast Wrap

Ingredients:

- 1 whole grain tortilla
- 1/2 cup sautéed spinach
- 1/4 cup sliced mushrooms
- 1/4 cup diced tomatoes
- 2 tablespoons hummus

Instructions:

I. Heat tortilla in a skillet until warm.
II. Spread hummus evenly onto tortilla.
III. Layer spinach, mushrooms, and diced tomatoes on top.
IV. Roll up the tortilla and serve.

Nutrient Value (per serving):

- Calories: 220
- Carbohydrates: 30g
- Protein: 7g
- Fat: 9g
- Fiber: 6g

9. Quinoa Breakfast Bowl

Ingredients:

- 1/2 cup cooked quinoa
- 1/2 cup mixed berries
- 1/4 cup sliced almonds
- 1 tablespoon maple syrup or agave nectar

Instructions:

I. In a bowl, combine cooked quinoa, mixed berries, and sliced almonds.
II. Drizzle with maple syrup or agave nectar.
III. Stir gently to combine and serve.

Nutrient Value (per serving):

- Calories: 280
- Carbohydrates: 40g
- Protein: 8g
- Fat: 10g
- Fiber: 6g

10. Blueberry Oat Pancakes

Ingredients:

- 1 cup rolled oats
- 1 ripe banana
- 1/2 cup almond milk
- 1/2 cup blueberries
- 1 teaspoon vanilla extract

Instructions:

   I. In a blender, combine rolled oats, banana, almond milk, and vanilla extract.
   II. Blend until smooth.
   III. Fold in blueberries.
   IV. Heat a non-stick skillet over medium heat.
   V. Pour batter onto skillet to form pancakes.
   VI. Cook for 2-3 minutes on each side, until golden brown.
   VII. Serve with additional blueberries and maple syrup if desired.

Nutrient Value (per serving):

- Calories: 300
- Carbohydrates: 55g
- Protein: 8g
- Fat: 6g
- Fiber: 7g

Chapter 5

VEGAN TYPE 2 DIABETIC LUNCH RECIPES

1. Quinoa Salad with Roasted Vegetables

Ingredients:

- 1 cup quinoa
- Assorted vegetables (such as bell peppers, zucchini, and cherry tomatoes)
- Olive oil
- Salt and pepper
- Fresh herbs (such as parsley or basil)
- Balsamic vinegar (optional)

Instructions:

1. Cook quinoa according to package instructions and let it cool.
2. Chop vegetables into bite-sized pieces, toss with olive oil, salt, and pepper, and roast in the oven until tender.
3. Combine cooked quinoa with roasted vegetables, fresh herbs, and a drizzle of balsamic vinegar if desired.

Nutrient Value:

- High in fiber and protein from quinoa

- Rich in vitamins and minerals from assorted vegetables
- Provides healthy fats from olive oil

2. Chickpea and Vegetable Stir-Fry

Ingredients:

- 1 can chickpeas, drained and rinsed
- Assorted vegetables (such as broccoli, bell peppers, and carrots)
- Garlic, minced
- Ginger, grated
- Low-sodium soy sauce or tamari
- Sesame oil
- Brown rice or quinoa (optional)

Instructions:

1. Heat sesame oil in a pan and sauté minced garlic and grated ginger until fragrant.
2. Add assorted vegetables and chickpeas to the pan and stir-fry until vegetables are tender.
3. Season with low-sodium soy sauce or tamari to taste.
4. Serve over brown rice or quinoa if desired.

Nutrient Value:

- High in protein and fiber from chickpeas
- Provides vitamins and minerals from assorted vegetables
- Contains healthy fats from sesame oil

3. Lentil and Vegetable Soup

Ingredients:

- 1 cup lentils, rinsed
- Assorted vegetables (such as onions, carrots, celery, and spinach)
- Vegetable broth
- Garlic, minced
- Herbs and spices (such as thyme, rosemary, and bay leaves)
- Salt and pepper to taste

Instructions:

1. In a large pot, sauté minced garlic in olive oil until fragrant.
2. Add chopped vegetables and cook until softened.
3. Add lentils, vegetable broth, herbs, and spices to the pot and bring to a boil.
4. Reduce heat and simmer until lentils are tender.
5. Season with salt and pepper to taste before serving.

Nutrient Value:

- High in fiber and protein from lentils
- Provides vitamins and minerals from assorted vegetables
- Low in fat and calories

4. Tofu and Vegetable Stir-Fry

Ingredients:

- Firm tofu, cubed
- Assorted vegetables (such as bell peppers, broccoli, and snap peas)
- Low-sodium soy sauce or tamari
- Garlic, minced
- Ginger, grated
- Sesame oil
- Brown rice or quinoa (optional)

Instructions:

1. Heat sesame oil in a pan and sauté minced garlic and grated ginger until fragrant.
2. Add cubed tofu to the pan and cook until golden brown on all sides.
3. Add assorted vegetables and stir-fry until tender.
4. Season with low-sodium soy sauce or tamari to taste.

5. Serve over brown rice or quinoa if desired.

Nutrient Value:

- High in protein from tofu
- Provides vitamins and minerals from assorted vegetables
- Contains healthy fats from sesame oil

5. Black Bean and Sweet Potato Burrito Bowl

Ingredients:

- Cooked black beans
- Roasted sweet potatoes
- Cooked brown rice
- Avocado slices
- Salsa
- Cilantro, chopped
- Lime wedges

Instructions:

1. Assemble cooked black beans, roasted sweet potatoes, and cooked brown rice in a bowl.
2. Top with avocado slices, salsa, and chopped cilantro.
3. Serve with lime wedges for squeezing over the bowl.

Nutrient Value:

- High in fiber and protein from black beans
- Provides vitamins and minerals from sweet potatoes and avocado
- Contains healthy carbohydrates from brown rice

6. Mediterranean Chickpea Salad

Ingredients:

- Cooked chickpeas
- Cherry tomatoes, halved
- Cucumber, diced
- Red onion, thinly sliced
- Kalamata olives, pitted
- Fresh parsley, chopped
- Lemon juice
- Extra virgin olive oil
- Salt and pepper to taste

Instructions:

1. In a large bowl, combine chickpeas, cherry tomatoes, cucumber, red onion, and Kalamata olives.
2. Drizzle with lemon juice and extra virgin olive oil.
3. Season with salt and pepper to taste.
4. Garnish with chopped parsley before serving.

Nutrient Value:

- High in fiber and protein from chickpeas
- Provides vitamins and minerals from assorted vegetables and olives
- Contains healthy fats from extra virgin olive oil

7. Tofu Veggie Wrap

Ingredients:

- Whole grain tortillas
- Firm tofu, sliced
- Assorted vegetables (such as lettuce, bell peppers, carrots, and cucumbers)
- Hummus or avocado spread

Instructions:

1. Spread a layer of hummus or mashed avocado onto a whole grain tortilla.
2. Layer sliced tofu and assorted vegetables on top of the spread.
3. Roll up the tortilla tightly, tucking in the ends as you go.
4. Slice the wrap in half and serve.

Nutrient Value:

- High in protein from tofu
- Provides vitamins and minerals from assorted vegetables

- Contains healthy carbohydrates and fiber from whole grain tortillas

8. Roasted Vegetable and Hummus Sandwich
Ingredients:

- Whole grain bread
- Assorted roasted vegetables (such as eggplant, bell peppers, and zucchini)
- Hummus
- Fresh spinach leaves

Instructions:

1. Spread a layer of hummus onto whole grain bread slices.
2. Layer roasted vegetables and fresh spinach leaves on top of the hummus.
3. Close the sandwich with another slice of bread.
4. Slice the sandwich in half and serve.

Nutrient Value:

- Provides vitamins and minerals from roasted vegetables and spinach
- Contains healthy carbohydrates and fiber from whole grain bread
- Offers plant-based protein from hummus

9. Spinach and Mushroom Vegan Frittata

Ingredients:

- Chickpea flour
- Nutritional yeast
- Baking powder
- Garlic powder
- Onion powder
- Turmeric
- Spinach leaves
- Mushrooms, sliced
- Red bell pepper, diced
- Almond milk
- Salt and pepper to taste

Instructions:

1. Preheat the oven to 375°F (190°C) and grease a pie dish.
2. In a mixing bowl, combine chickpea flour, nutritional yeast, baking powder, garlic powder, onion powder, turmeric, almond milk, salt, and pepper to make the batter.
3. Stir in spinach leaves, sliced mushrooms, and diced red bell pepper.
4. Pour the batter into the greased pie dish and bake for 25-30 minutes, or until set and golden brown on top.
5. Allow the frittata to cool slightly before slicing and serving.

Nutrient Value:

- High in protein from chickpea flour
- Provides vitamins and minerals from spinach, mushrooms, and bell peppers
- Low in carbohydrates and suitable for blood sugar control

10. Stuffed Bell Peppers with Quinoa and Black Beans

- **Ingredients:**
- Bell peppers (assorted colors)
- Cooked quinoa
- Cooked black beans
- Corn kernels
- Diced tomatoes
- Onion, diced
- Garlic, minced
- Cumin, paprika, chili powder (to taste)
- Salt and pepper to taste
- Vegan cheese (optional)

Instructions:

1. Preheat the oven to 375°F (190°C) and prepare a baking dish.
2. Cut the tops off the bell peppers and remove the seeds and membranes.
3. In a skillet, sauté onion and garlic until softened. Add cooked quinoa, black beans,

corn, diced tomatoes, and spices. Cook until heated through.
4. Stuff the bell peppers with the quinoa and black bean mixture, pressing down gently to fill each pepper.
5. If desired, top each stuffed pepper with vegan cheese.
6. Place the stuffed peppers in the prepared baking dish and bake for 25-30 minutes, or until the peppers are tender.
7. Serve hot.

Nutrient Value:

- High in fiber and protein from quinoa and black beans
- Provides vitamins and minerals from assorted vegetables
- Low in fat and suitable for blood sugar control

Chapter 6

VEGANS TYPE 2 DIABETIC DINNER RECIPES:

1. Quinoa-Stuffed Bell Peppers

Ingredients:

- Bell peppers
- Quinoa
- Black beans
- Corn
- Diced tomatoes
- Onion
- Garlic
- Spices (cumin, chili powder, paprika)

Instructions:

1. Preheat oven to 375°F (190°C).
2. Cook quinoa according to package instructions.
3. In a skillet, sauté onion and garlic until softened.
4. Mix cooked quinoa, black beans, corn, diced tomatoes, onion, garlic, and spices in a bowl.
5. Cut tops off bell peppers, remove seeds, and stuff with quinoa mixture.

6. Place stuffed peppers in a baking dish, cover with foil, and bake for 25-30 minutes.

Nutrient Value (per serving):

- Calories: 250
- Carbohydrates: 45g
- Protein: 10g
- Fat: 3g
- Fiber: 10g

2. Lentil Vegetable Soup

Ingredients:

- Lentils
- Carrots
- Celery
- Onion
- Garlic
- Vegetable broth
- Spinach
- Tomatoes
- Bay leaves
- Herbs (thyme, rosemary, parsley)

Instructions:

1. In a large pot, sauté onion and garlic until translucent.

2. Add chopped carrots, celery, lentils, tomatoes, vegetable broth, bay leaves, and herbs.
3. Bring to a boil, then reduce heat and simmer for 20-25 minutes until lentils are tender.
4. Stir in spinach and cook until wilted.
5. Season with salt and pepper to taste before serving.

Nutrient Value (per serving):

- Calories: 200
- Carbohydrates: 35g
- Protein: 12g
- Fat: 1g
- Fiber: 12g

3. Chickpea and Vegetable Stir-Fry

Ingredients:

- Chickpeas
- Bell peppers
- Broccoli
- Carrots
- Snap peas
- Onion
- Garlic
- Soy sauce (or tamari for gluten-free option)
- Ginger
- Rice vinegar

- Sesame oil

Instructions:

1. Heat sesame oil in a wok or large skillet over medium-high heat.
2. Add chopped onion, garlic, and ginger, and stir-fry for 1-2 minutes.
3. Add chopped vegetables and chickpeas, and continue stir-frying until vegetables are tender-crisp.
4. Stir in soy sauce and rice vinegar, and cook for another minute.
5. Serve hot over cooked brown rice or quinoa.

Nutrient Value (per serving):

- Calories: 280
- Carbohydrates: 45g
- Protein: 14g
- Fat: 5g
- Fiber: 12g

4. Spaghetti Squash with Marinara Sauce

Ingredients:

- Spaghetti squash
- Tomatoes
- Onion
- Garlic
- Olive oil

- Basil
- Oregano
- Salt and pepper

Instructions:

1. Preheat oven to 400°F (200°C).
2. Cut spaghetti squash in half lengthwise, remove seeds, and place cut-side down on a baking sheet.
3. Roast squash for 40-50 minutes until tender.
4. Meanwhile, sauté chopped onion and garlic in olive oil until softened.
5. Add chopped tomatoes, basil, oregano, salt, and pepper, and simmer for 20-25 minutes.
6. Scrape the flesh of the cooked spaghetti squash with a fork to create "spaghetti" strands.
7. Serve squash topped with marinara sauce.

Nutrient Value (per serving):

- Calories: 180
- Carbohydrates: 35g
- Protein: 5g
- Fat: 4g
- Fiber: 8g

5. Tofu and Vegetable Stir-Fry with Brown Rice

Ingredients:

- Firm tofu
- Broccoli
- Bell peppers
- Carrots
- Snap peas
- Onion
- Garlic
- Soy sauce (or tamari for gluten-free option)
- Ginger
- Cornstarch
- Brown rice

Instructions:

1. Press tofu to remove excess moisture, then cut into cubes.
2. Heat oil in a wok or large skillet over medium-high heat.
3. Add tofu cubes and cook until golden brown on all sides, then remove from pan and set aside.
4. In the same pan, sauté chopped onion, garlic, and ginger until fragrant.
5. Add chopped vegetables and stir-fry until tender-crisp.
6. In a small bowl, whisk together soy sauce and cornstarch, then pour over vegetables.

7. Add cooked tofu back to the pan and toss to combine.
8. Serve hot over cooked brown rice.

Nutrient Value (per serving):

- Calories: 320
- Carbohydrates: 45g
- Protein: 18g
- Fat: 8g
- Fiber: 10g

6. Mushroom and Spinach Risotto

Ingredients:

- Arborio rice
- Mushrooms
- Spinach
- Onion
- Garlic
- Vegetable broth
- White wine (optional)
- Nutritional yeast
- Olive oil
- Thyme

Instructions:

1. In a large pot, heat olive oil over medium heat.

Vegan Type-2 Diabetic Diet Cookbook

2. Sauté chopped onion and garlic until translucent.
3. Add Arborio rice and cook for 1-2 minutes until lightly toasted.
4. Deglaze the pot with white wine (if using) and cook until absorbed.
5. Gradually add vegetable broth, stirring constantly, until rice is cooked and creamy.
6. In a separate skillet, sauté sliced mushrooms until golden brown.
7. Stir cooked mushrooms and fresh spinach into the risotto.
8. Season with nutritional yeast, thyme, salt, and pepper before serving.

Nutrient Value (per serving):

- Calories: 300
- Carbohydrates: 50g
- Protein: 10g
- Fat: 5g
- Fiber: 6g

7. Veggie Burger with Sweet Potato Fries
Ingredients:

- Vegan burger patties
- Whole grain burger buns
- Sweet potatoes
- Olive oil

- Paprika
- Garlic powder
- Salt and pepper
- Lettuce, tomato, avocado (for topping)

Instructions:

1. Preheat oven to 425°F (220°C).
2. Slice sweet potatoes into fries, toss with olive oil, paprika, garlic powder, salt, and pepper, and spread on a baking sheet.
3. Bake sweet potato fries for 20-25 minutes until crispy.
4. Cook vegan burger patties according to package instructions.
5. Assemble burgers with whole grain buns, lettuce, tomato, avocado, and any other desired toppings.
6. Serve burgers with sweet potato fries on the side.

Nutrient Value (per serving):

- Calories: 380
- Carbohydrates: 50g
- Protein: 15g
- Fat: 10g
- Fiber: 10g

8. Chickpea and Vegetable Curry

Ingredients:

- Chickpeas
- Cauliflower
- Carrots
- Bell peppers
- Onion
- Garlic
- Ginger
- Coconut milk
- Curry powder
- Turmeric
- Cumin
- Coriander
- Cilantro (for garnish)

Instructions:

1. In a large pot, sauté chopped onion, garlic, and ginger until softened.
2. Add chopped vegetables, chickpeas, and spices, and stir to coat.
3. Pour in coconut milk and bring to a simmer.
4. Cook for 15-20 minutes until vegetables are tender and flavors are well combined.
5. Serve hot, garnished with chopped cilantro, over cooked brown rice or quinoa.

Nutrient Value (per serving):

- Calories: 320
- Carbohydrates: 45g
- Protein: 12g
- Fat: 10g
- Fiber: 12g

9. Vegan Chili with Beans and Lentils

Ingredients:

- Black beans
- Kidney beans
- Lentils
- Tomatoes
- Bell peppers
- Onion
- Garlic
- Vegetable broth
- Chili powder
- Cumin
- Paprika
- Cayenne pepper (optional)

Instructions:

1. In a large pot, sauté chopped onion and garlic until fragrant.
2. Add chopped bell peppers, tomatoes, beans, lentils, vegetable broth, and spices.

3. Bring to a boil, then reduce heat and simmer for 30-40 minutes until flavors meld together.
4. Adjust seasoning to taste, adding more chili powder or cayenne pepper for extra heat if desired.
5. Serve hot, optionally topped with diced avocado, cilantro, or vegan sour cream.

Nutrient Value (per serving):

- Calories: 300
- Carbohydrates: 50g
- Protein: 15g
- Fat: 2g
- Fiber: 15g

10. Roasted Vegetable and Quinoa Salad

Ingredients:

- Quinoa
- Zucchini
- Eggplant
- Cherry tomatoes
- Red onion
- Bell peppers
- Garlic
- Olive oil
- Balsamic vinegar
- Fresh basil
- Salt and pepper

Instructions:

1. Preheat oven to 400°F (200°C).
2. Cook quinoa according to package instructions.
3. Chop zucchini, eggplant, cherry tomatoes, red onion, and bell peppers into bite-sized pieces.
4. Toss chopped vegetables with minced garlic, olive oil, balsamic vinegar, salt, and pepper.
5. Spread vegetables on a baking sheet and roast for 25-30 minutes until tender and caramelized.
6. In a large bowl, combine cooked quinoa with roasted vegetables and chopped fresh basil.
7. Serve warm or at room temperature as a satisfying and nutritious salad.

Nutrient Value (per serving):

- Calories: 280
- Carbohydrates: 45g
- Protein: 10g
- Fat: 6g
- Fiber: 10g

Chapter 7

Vegans Type 2 Diabetic Dinner Recipes:

1. Quinoa-Stuffed Bell Peppers

Ingredients:

- Bell peppers
- Quinoa
- Black beans
- Corn
- Diced tomatoes
- Onion
- Garlic
- Spices (cumin, chili powder, paprika)

Instructions:

1. Preheat oven to 375°F (190°C).
2. Cook quinoa according to package instructions.
3. In a skillet, sauté onion and garlic until softened.
4. Mix cooked quinoa, black beans, corn, diced tomatoes, onion, garlic, and spices in a bowl.
5. Cut tops off bell peppers, remove seeds, and stuff with quinoa mixture.
6. Place stuffed peppers in a baking dish, cover with foil, and bake for 25-30 minutes.

Nutrient Value (per serving):

- Calories: 250
- Carbohydrates: 45g
- Protein: 10g
- Fat: 3g
- Fiber: 10g

2. Lentil Vegetable Soup

Ingredients:

- Lentils
- Carrots
- Celery
- Onion
- Garlic
- Vegetable broth
- Spinach
- Tomatoes
- Bay leaves
- Herbs (thyme, rosemary, parsley)

Instructions:

1. In a large pot, sauté onion and garlic until translucent.
2. Add chopped carrots, celery, lentils, tomatoes, vegetable broth, bay leaves, and herbs.

3. Bring to a boil, then reduce heat and simmer for 20-25 minutes until lentils are tender.
4. Stir in spinach and cook until wilted.
5. Season with salt and pepper to taste before serving.

Nutrient Value (per serving):

- Calories: 200
- Carbohydrates: 35g
- Protein: 12g
- Fat: 1g
- Fiber: 12g

3. Chickpea and Vegetable Stir-Fry

Ingredients:

- Chickpeas
- Bell peppers
- Broccoli
- Carrots
- Snap peas
- Onion
- Garlic
- Soy sauce (or tamari for gluten-free option)
- Ginger
- Rice vinegar
- Sesame oil

Instructions:

1. Heat sesame oil in a wok or large skillet over medium-high heat.
2. Add chopped onion, garlic, and ginger, and stir-fry for 1-2 minutes.
3. Add chopped vegetables and chickpeas, and continue stir-frying until vegetables are tender-crisp.
4. Stir in soy sauce and rice vinegar, and cook for another minute.
5. Serve hot over cooked brown rice or quinoa.

Nutrient Value (per serving):

- Calories: 280
- Carbohydrates: 45g
- Protein: 14g
- Fat: 5g
- Fiber: 12g

4. Spaghetti Squash with Marinara Sauce

Ingredients:

- Spaghetti squash
- Tomatoes
- Onion
- Garlic
- Olive oil

- Basil
- Oregano
- Salt and pepper

Instructions:

1. Preheat oven to 400°F (200°C).
2. Cut spaghetti squash in half lengthwise, remove seeds, and place cut-side down on a baking sheet.
3. Roast squash for 40-50 minutes until tender.
4. Meanwhile, sauté chopped onion and garlic in olive oil until softened.
5. Add chopped tomatoes, basil, oregano, salt, and pepper, and simmer for 20-25 minutes.
6. Scrape the flesh of the cooked spaghetti squash with a fork to create "spaghetti" strands.
7. Serve squash topped with marinara sauce.

Nutrient Value (per serving):

- Calories: 180
- Carbohydrates: 35g
- Protein: 5g
- Fat: 4g
- Fiber: 8g

5. Tofu and Vegetable Stir-Fry with Brown Rice

Ingredients:

- Firm tofu
- Broccoli
- Bell peppers
- Carrots
- Snap peas
- Onion
- Garlic
- Soy sauce (or tamari for gluten-free option)
- Ginger
- Cornstarch
- Brown rice

Instructions:

1. Press tofu to remove excess moisture, then cut into cubes.
2. Heat oil in a wok or large skillet over medium-high heat.
3. Add tofu cubes and cook until golden brown on all sides, then remove from pan and set aside.
4. In the same pan, sauté chopped onion, garlic, and ginger until fragrant.
5. Add chopped vegetables and stir-fry until tender-crisp.
6. In a small bowl, whisk together soy sauce and cornstarch, then pour over vegetables.

7. Add cooked tofu back to the pan and toss to combine.
8. Serve hot over cooked brown rice.

Nutrient Value (per serving):

- Calories: 320
- Carbohydrates: 45g
- Protein: 18g
- Fat: 8g
- Fiber: 10g

6. Mushroom and Spinach Risotto

Ingredients:

- Arborio rice
- Mushrooms
- Spinach
- Onion
- Garlic
- Vegetable broth
- White wine (optional)
- Nutritional yeast
- Olive oil
- Thyme

Instructions:

1. In a large pot, heat olive oil over medium heat.

2. Sauté chopped onion and garlic until translucent.
3. Add Arborio rice and cook for 1-2 minutes until lightly toasted.
4. Deglaze the pot with white wine (if using) and cook until absorbed.
5. Gradually add vegetable broth, stirring constantly, until rice is cooked and creamy.
6. In a separate skillet, sauté sliced mushrooms until golden brown.
7. Stir cooked mushrooms and fresh spinach into the risotto.
8. Season with nutritional yeast, thyme, salt, and pepper before serving.

Nutrient Value (per serving):

- Calories: 300
- Carbohydrates: 50g
- Protein: 10g
- Fat: 5g
- Fiber: 6g

7. Veggie Burger with Sweet Potato Fries
Ingredients:

- Vegan burger patties
- Whole grain burger buns
- Sweet potatoes

- Olive oil
- Paprika
- Garlic powder
- Salt and pepper
- Lettuce, tomato, avocado (for topping)

Instructions:

1. Preheat oven to 425°F (220°C).
2. Slice sweet potatoes into fries, toss with olive oil, paprika, garlic powder, salt, and pepper, and spread on a baking sheet.
3. Bake sweet potato fries for 20-25 minutes until crispy.
4. Cook vegan burger patties according to package instructions.
5. Assemble burgers with whole grain buns, lettuce, tomato, avocado, and any other desired toppings.
6. Serve burgers with sweet potato fries on the side.

Nutrient Value (per serving):

- Calories: 380
- Carbohydrates: 50g
- Protein: 15g
- Fat: 10g
- Fiber: 10g

8. Chickpea and Vegetable Curry

Ingredients:

- Chickpeas
- Cauliflower
- Carrots
- Bell peppers
- Onion
- Garlic
- Ginger
- Coconut milk
- Curry powder
- Turmeric
- Cumin
- Coriander
- Cilantro (for garnish)

Instructions:

1. In a large pot, sauté chopped onion, garlic, and ginger until softened.
2. Add chopped vegetables, chickpeas, and spices, and stir to coat.
3. Pour in coconut milk and bring to a simmer.
4. Cook for 15-20 minutes until vegetables are tender and flavors are well combined.
5. Serve hot, garnished with chopped cilantro, over cooked brown rice or quinoa.

Nutrient Value (per serving):

- Calories: 320
- Carbohydrates: 45g
- Protein: 12g
- Fat: 10g
- Fiber: 12g

9. Vegan Chili with Beans and Lentils

Ingredients:

- Black beans
- Kidney beans
- Lentils
- Tomatoes
- Bell peppers
- Onion
- Garlic
- Vegetable broth
- Chili powder
- Cumin
- Paprika
- Cayenne pepper (optional)

Instructions:

1. In a large pot, sauté chopped onion and garlic until fragrant.

2. Add chopped bell peppers, tomatoes, beans, lentils, vegetable broth, and spices.
3. Bring to a boil, then reduce heat and simmer for 30-40 minutes until flavors meld together.
4. Adjust seasoning to taste, adding more chili powder or cayenne pepper for extra heat if desired.
5. Serve hot, optionally topped with diced avocado, cilantro, or vegan sour cream.

Nutrient Value (per serving):

- Calories: 300
- Carbohydrates: 50g
- Protein: 15g
- Fat: 2g
- Fiber: 15g

10. Roasted Vegetable and Quinoa Salad

Ingredients:

- Quinoa
- Zucchini
- Eggplant
- Cherry tomatoes
- Red onion
- Bell peppers
- Garlic
- Olive oil

- Balsamic vinegar
- Fresh basil
- Salt and pepper

Instructions:

1. Preheat oven to 400°F (200°C).
2. Cook quinoa according to package instructions.
3. Chop zucchini, eggplant, cherry tomatoes, red onion, and bell peppers into bite-sized pieces.
4. Toss chopped vegetables with minced garlic, olive oil, balsamic vinegar, salt, and pepper.
5. Spread vegetables on a baking sheet and roast for 25-30 minutes until tender and caramelized.
6. In a large bowl, combine cooked quinoa with roasted vegetables and chopped fresh basil.
7. Serve warm or at room temperature as a satisfying and nutritious salad.

Nutrient Value (per serving):

- Calories: 280
- Carbohydrates: 45g
- Protein: 10g
- Fat: 6g
- Fiber: 10g

Chapter 8

VEGANS TYPE 2 DIABETIC SNACK RECIPES:

1. Chickpea Salad

Ingredients:

- 1 can chickpeas, drained and rinsed
- 1 cucumber, diced
- 1 tomato, diced
- 1/4 cup red onion, finely chopped
- 2 tablespoons fresh parsley, chopped
- Juice of 1 lemon
- Salt and pepper to taste

Instructions:

1. In a large bowl, combine chickpeas, cucumber, tomato, red onion, and parsley.
2. Drizzle with lemon juice and season with salt and pepper.
3. Toss until well combined. Serve chilled.

Nutrient Value: High in fiber, protein, and vitamins C and K.

2. Almond Butter Apple Slices

Ingredients:

- 1 apple, sliced
- 2 tablespoons almond butter
- Optional toppings: cinnamon, shredded coconut
- Instructions:
- Spread almond butter on apple slices.
- Sprinkle with cinnamon and shredded coconut if desired.

Nutrient Value: Rich in fiber, healthy fats, and vitamin C.

3. Edamame Hummus with Carrot Sticks

Ingredients:

- 1 cup shelled edamame, cooked
- 2 tablespoons tahini
- 1 garlic clove
- Juice of 1 lemon
- 1 tablespoon olive oil
- Salt and pepper to taste
- Carrot sticks for dipping

Instructions:

1. In a food processor, combine edamame, tahini, garlic, lemon juice, olive oil, salt, and pepper.

2. Blend until smooth and creamy.
3. Serve with carrot sticks for dipping.

Nutrient Value: High in protein, fiber, and healthy fats.

4. Roasted Chickpeas

Ingredients:

- 1 can chickpeas, drained and rinsed
- 1 tablespoon olive oil
- 1 teaspoon paprika
- 1/2 teaspoon garlic powder
- Salt to taste

Instructions:

1. Preheat oven to 400°F (200°C).
2. Pat chickpeas dry with a paper towel and place on a baking sheet.
3. Drizzle with olive oil and sprinkle with paprika, garlic powder, and salt. Toss to coat.
4. Bake for 20-25 minutes, or until crispy, stirring halfway through.

Nutrient Value: Rich in protein, fiber, and iron.

5. Berry Chia Pudding

Ingredients:

- 1/4 cup chia seeds
- 1 cup unsweetened almond milk
- 1/2 cup mixed berries (strawberries, blueberries, raspberries)
- 1 tablespoon maple syrup (optional)

Instructions:

1. In a jar or bowl, mix chia seeds and almond milk. Let sit for 5 minutes, and then stir again.
2. Cover and refrigerate for at least 2 hours or overnight, until thickened.
3. Serve topped with mixed berries and a drizzle of maple syrup if desired.

Nutrient Value: High in fiber, omega-3 fatty acids, and antioxidants.

6. Vegetable Sushi Rolls

Ingredients:

- Nori sheets
- Cooked sushi rice
- Assorted vegetables (cucumber, avocado, bell pepper, carrot)
- Soy sauce or tamari for dipping

Instructions:

1. Place a nori sheet on a bamboo sushi mat.
2. Spread a layer of sushi rice over the nori, leaving a border along the edges.
3. Arrange thinly sliced vegetables in the center of the rice.
4. Roll up the nori tightly using the sushi mat.
5. Slice into bite-sized pieces and serve with soy sauce or tamari for dipping.

Nutrient Value: Low in calories, rich in fiber, vitamins, and minerals.

7. Greek Yogurt with Berries and Almonds

Ingredients:

- 1/2 cup unsweetened coconut or almond yogurt
- 1/4 cup mixed berries (blueberries, strawberries, raspberries)
- 1 tablespoon sliced almonds
- Drizzle of honey or maple syrup (optional)

Instructions:

1. In a bowl, layer yogurt, mixed berries, and sliced almonds.
2. Drizzle with honey or maple syrup if desired.

Nutrient Value: High in protein, fiber, and antioxidants.

8. Spicy Roasted Cauliflower

Ingredients:

- 1 head cauliflower, cut into florets
- 1 tablespoon olive oil
- 1 teaspoon smoked paprika
- 1/2 teaspoon cumin
- 1/4 teaspoon cayenne pepper
- Salt to taste

Instructions:

1. Preheat oven to 425°F (220°C).
2. In a large bowl, toss cauliflower florets with olive oil, smoked paprika, cumin, cayenne pepper, and salt.
3. Spread evenly on a baking sheet and roast for 25-30 minutes, or until golden brown and crispy.

Nutrient Value: Low in calories, rich in fiber, vitamin C, and antioxidants.

9. Stuffed Mini Bell Peppers

Ingredients:

- Mini bell peppers, halved and seeded
- Hummus or vegan cream cheese
- Sliced cucumber, cherry tomatoes, or olives for topping

Instructions:

1. Fill each mini bell pepper half with hummus or vegan cream cheese.
2. Top with sliced cucumber, cherry tomatoes, or olives.

Nutrient Value: High in fiber, vitamins, and minerals.

10. Trail Mix

Ingredients:

- 1/4 cup almonds
- 1/4 cup walnuts
- 1/4 cup pumpkin seeds
- 1/4 cup dried cranberries
- 1/4 cup dark chocolate chips (optional)

Instructions:

1. In a bowl, combine almonds, walnuts, pumpkin seeds, dried cranberries, and dark chocolate chips.
2. Mix well and portion into individual snack bags for on-the-go convenience.

Nutrient Value: High in protein, healthy fats, and antioxidants.

Chapter 9

DESSERTS AND TREATS FOR TYPE 2 DIABETICS

1. Chia Seed Pudding

Ingredients:

- 2 tablespoons chia seeds
- 1 cup unsweetened almond milk
- 1/2 teaspoon vanilla extract
- Stevia or erythritol to taste
- Fresh berries for topping

Instructions:

1. In a bowl, mix chia seeds, almond milk, vanilla extract, and sweetener.
2. Refrigerate for at least 2 hours or overnight until the mixture thickens.
3. Serve chilled, topped with fresh berries.

Nutrient Value (per serving):

- Calories: 120
- Carbohydrates: 12g
- Fiber: 8g
- Protein: 4g

2. Baked Apples

Ingredients:

- 2 medium apples, cored
- 1 tablespoon chopped walnuts
- 1/2 teaspoon cinnamon
- 1 teaspoon honey or maple syrup (optional)

Instructions:

1. Preheat the oven to 375°F (190°C).
2. In a small bowl, mix chopped walnuts and cinnamon.
3. Stuff each apple with the walnut mixture.
4. Drizzle honey or maple syrup over the apples if desired.
5. Place the stuffed apples in a baking dish and bake for 25-30 minutes until tender.
6. Serve warm.

Nutrient Value (per serving, without honey/maple syrup):

- Calories: 120
- Carbohydrates: 20g
- Fiber: 5g
- Protein: 2g

3. Greek Yogurt Parfait

Ingredients:

- 1/2 cup plain Greek yogurt
- 1/4 cup fresh berries
- 1 tablespoon chopped nuts (such as almonds or walnuts)
- 1 teaspoon honey or stevia (optional)

Instructions:

1. In a glass, layer Greek yogurt, fresh berries, and chopped nuts.
2. Drizzle honey or sprinkle stevia on top if desired.
3. Repeat the layers if making multiple servings.
4. Serve immediately.

Nutrient Value (per serving, without honey):

- Calories: 150
- Carbohydrates: 10g
- Fiber: 2g
- Protein: 12g

4. Dark Chocolate-Dipped Strawberries

Ingredients:

- 10 large strawberries, washed and dried
- 2 ounces dark chocolate (70% cocoa or higher)

Instructions:

1. Line a baking sheet with parchment paper.
2. In a microwave-safe bowl, melt the dark chocolate in 30-second intervals, stirring between each interval until smooth.
3. Dip each strawberry into the melted chocolate, coating about halfway.
4. Place the dipped strawberries on the prepared baking sheet.
5. Refrigerate for 20-30 minutes until the chocolate sets.
6. Serve chilled.

Nutrient Value (per serving, based on 2 strawberries):

- Calories: 60
- Carbohydrates: 7g
- Fiber: 2g
- Protein: 1g

5. Coconut Flour Banana Muffins

Ingredients:

- 2 ripe bananas, mashed
- 2 eggs
- 1/4 cup coconut flour
- 1/4 cup unsweetened almond milk
- 1 teaspoon baking powder
- 1/2 teaspoon cinnamon
- 1/4 teaspoon salt
- Stevia or erythritol to taste (optional)

Instructions:

1. Preheat the oven to 350°F (175°C). Line a muffin tin with paper liners.
2. In a bowl, mix mashed bananas, eggs, almond milk, and sweetener (if using).
3. In a separate bowl, whisk together coconut flour, baking powder, cinnamon, and salt.
4. Gradually add the dry ingredients to the wet ingredients, stirring until well combined.
5. Divide the batter evenly among the muffin cups.
6. Bake for 20-25 minutes until a toothpick inserted into the center comes out clean.
7. Allow the muffins to cool before serving.

Nutrient Value (per muffin, without sweetener):

- Calories: 80
- Carbohydrates: 10g
- Fiber: 3g
- Protein: 4g

6. Avocado Chocolate Mousse

Ingredients:

- 1 ripe avocado
- 2 tablespoons unsweetened cocoa powder
- 2 tablespoons almond milk
- 1 tablespoon honey or maple syrup (optional)
- 1/2 teaspoon vanilla extract

Instructions:

1. Scoop the flesh of the avocado into a blender or food processor.
2. Add cocoa powder, almond milk, honey or maple syrup (if using), and vanilla extract.
3. Blend until smooth and creamy, scraping down the sides as needed.
4. Transfer the mousse to serving bowls and refrigerate for at least 30 minutes before serving.
5. Garnish with shaved dark chocolate or fresh berries if desired.

Nutrient Value (per serving, without sweetener):

- Calories: 150
- Carbohydrates: 10g
- Fiber: 7g
- Protein: 3g

7. Cinnamon Baked Pears

Ingredients:

- 2 ripe pears, halved and cored
- 1 tablespoon chopped walnuts
- 1/2 teaspoon cinnamon
- 1 teaspoon honey or maple syrup (optional)

Instructions:

1. Preheat the oven to 375°F (190°C). Line a baking dish with parchment paper.
2. Place pear halves cut side up in the baking dish.
3. In a small bowl, mix chopped walnuts and cinnamon.
4. Sprinkle the walnut-cinnamon mixture over the pear halves.
5. Drizzle honey or maple syrup over the pears if desired.

6. Bake for 25-30 minutes until the pears are tender and caramelized.
7. Serve warm.

Nutrient Value (per serving, without honey/maple syrup):

- Calories: 100
- Carbohydrates: 20g
- Fiber: 5g
- Protein: 1g

8. Peanut Butter Banana Bites

Ingredients:

- 1 medium banana, sliced
- 2 tablespoons natural peanut butter
- 2 tablespoons unsweetened shredded coconut

Instructions:

1. Spread peanut butter on banana slices.
2. Sandwich two banana slices together to form bites.
3. Roll the edges of the banana bites in shredded coconut.
4. Repeat with remaining banana slices.
5. Serve immediately or refrigerate for later.

Nutrient Value (per serving):

- Calories: 130
- Carbohydrates: 12g
- Fiber: 2g
- Protein: 3g

9. Berry Yogurt Bark

Ingredients:

- 1 cup plain Greek yogurt
- 1 tablespoon honey or maple syrup
- 1/2 cup mixed berries (such as strawberries, blueberries, raspberries)

Instructions:

1. Line a baking sheet with parchment paper.
2. In a bowl, mix Greek yogurt and honey or maple syrup.
3. Spread the yogurt mixture evenly onto the parchment paper.
4. Sprinkle mixed berries over the yogurt.
5. Freeze for 2-3 hours until firm.
6. Break the yogurt bark into pieces and serve immediately.

Nutrient Value (per serving):

- Calories: 70
- Carbohydrates: 8g
- Fiber: 1g

- Protein: 7g

10. Almond Flour Chocolate Chip Cookies

Ingredients:

- 1 cup almond flour
- 1/4 cup coconut oil, melted
- 1/4 cup sugar-free chocolate chips
- 1/4 cup erythritol or stevia
- 1 egg
- 1/2 teaspoon baking soda
- 1/2 teaspoon vanilla extract
- Pinch of salt

Instructions:

1. Preheat the oven to 350°F (175°C). Line a baking sheet with parchment paper.
2. In a bowl, mix almond flour, erythritol or stevia, baking soda, and salt.
3. Stir in melted coconut oil, egg, and vanilla extract until well combined.
4. Fold in sugar-free chocolate chips.
5. Drop spoonfuls of dough onto the prepared baking sheet.
6. Flatten the dough slightly with a fork.
7. Bake for 10-12 minutes until golden brown around the edges.

8. Allow the cookies to cool on the baking sheet for 5 minutes before transferring to a wire rack to cool completely.

Nutrient Value (per cookie):

- Calories: 90
- Carbohydrates: 5g
- Fiber: 1g
- Protein: 2g

Chapter 10

BEVERAGE OPTIONS SUITABLE FOR INDIVIDUALS WITH TYPE 2 DIABETES

1. Green Tea with Lemon:

Ingredients: Green tea bag, hot water, lemon slice.

Instructions: Steep the green tea bag in hot water for 3-5 minutes. Add a slice of lemon for flavor.

Nutrient Value: Green tea is rich in antioxidants and has minimal calories and carbohydrates. Lemon adds a refreshing citrus flavor and a small amount of vitamin C.

2. Golden Milk:

Ingredients: Unsweetened almond milk, ground turmeric, ground cinnamon, ground ginger, black pepper, sweetener (optional).

Instructions: Heat almond milk in a saucepan, whisk in turmeric, cinnamon, ginger, and a pinch of black pepper. Sweeten to taste if desired.

Nutrient Value: Turmeric contains curcumin, a compound with anti-inflammatory properties. Almond milk is low in carbohydrates and calories.

3. Berry Smoothie:

Ingredients: Frozen mixed berries (strawberries, blueberries, raspberries), unsweetened almond milk, spinach, chia seeds.

Instructions: Blend frozen berries, almond milk, and spinach until smooth. Stir in chia seeds for added fiber.

Nutrient Value: Berries are rich in antioxidants and fiber, while almond milk provides calcium and vitamin E. Chia seeds are a good source of omega-3 fatty acids and protein.

4. Cucumber Mint Infused Water:

Ingredients: Sliced cucumber, fresh mint leaves, water, ice cubes.

Instructions: Place cucumber slices and mint leaves in a pitcher of water. Let it infuse in the refrigerator for at least 1 hour before serving over ice.

Nutrient Value: Cucumber is low in carbohydrates and calories, while mint adds a refreshing flavor without any additional calories.

5. Coconut Water with Lime:

Ingredients: Unsweetened coconut water, lime juice.

Instructions: Combine coconut water and lime juice in a glass. Stir well and serve chilled.

Nutrient Value: Coconut water is naturally low in carbohydrates and calories, while lime juice provides vitamin C and adds a tangy flavor.

6. Iced Green Tea with Mint:

Ingredients: Green tea bags, hot water, fresh mint leaves, ice cubes.

Instructions: Steep green tea bags in hot water for 3-5 minutes. Add fresh mint leaves and let it cool. Serve over ice.

Nutrient Value: Green tea offers antioxidants, while mint provides a refreshing flavor without added calories or carbohydrates.

7. Almond Butter Protein Shake:

Ingredients: Unsweetened almond milk, unsweetened protein powder (plant-based), almond butter, ice cubes.

Instructions: Blend almond milk, protein powder, almond butter, and ice cubes until smooth.

Nutrient Value: Almond milk is low in carbohydrates and calories, while almond butter adds healthy fats and protein for satiety.

8. Hibiscus Iced Tea:

Ingredients: Dried hibiscus flowers, hot water, lemon slices, sweetener (optional), ice cubes.

Instructions: Steep dried hibiscus flowers in hot water for 10-15 minutes. Add lemon slices and sweetener if desired. Chill and serve over ice.

Nutrient Value: Hibiscus tea may help lower blood pressure, and lemon adds vitamin C and flavor.

9. Sparkling Water with Citrus:

Ingredients: Sparkling water, lemon or lime slices.

Instructions: Pour sparkling water into a glass and add lemon or lime slices for flavor.

Nutrient Value: Sparkling water is calorie-free and refreshing, while lemon or lime slices add vitamin C without adding sugar or calories.

10. Ginger Turmeric Lemonade:

Ingredients: Water, fresh ginger slices, ground turmeric, lemon juice, sweetener (optional), ice cubes.

Instructions: Boil water with ginger slices and turmeric for 5 minutes. Strain, then add lemon juice and sweetener if desired. Chill and serve over ice.

Nutrient Value: Ginger and turmeric offer anti-inflammatory properties, while lemon provides vitamin C. Adjust sweetener to control carbohydrate intake.

Chapter 11

4-WEEK MEAL PLAN FOR TYPE 2 DIABETES REVERSAL

Week 1: Breakfast, Lunch, Dinner, and Snack Ideas

Day 1:

Breakfast: Overnight oats with chia seeds, almond milk, and mixed berries.

Lunch: Quinoa salad with mixed vegetables, chickpeas, and lemon-tahini dressing.

Dinner: Baked salmon with roasted sweet potatoes and steamed broccoli.

Snack: Apple slices with almond butter.

Day 2:

Breakfast: Spinach and mushroom tofu scramble with whole grain toast.

Lunch: Lentil soup with a side of mixed green salad.

Dinner: Stir-fried tofu with vegetables and brown rice.

Snack: Carrot sticks with hummus.

Day 3:

Breakfast: Whole grain toast with avocado slices and cherry tomatoes.

Lunch: Black bean tacos with corn tortillas, salsa, and guacamole.

Dinner: Grilled chicken breast with quinoa pilaf and sautéed spinach.

Snack: Greek yogurt with sliced strawberries.

Week 2: Meal Plan for Variety and Balanced Nutrition

Day 1:

Breakfast: Berry smoothie with spinach, almond milk, and protein powder.

Lunch: Mediterranean quinoa salad with cucumbers, tomatoes, olives, and feta cheese.

Dinner: Baked tofu with roasted Brussels sprouts and wild rice.

Snack: Mixed nuts and dried fruit.

Day 2:

Breakfast: Whole grain pancakes with banana slices and maple syrup.

Lunch: Vegetable stir-fry with tofu and brown rice.

Dinner: Lentil curry with cauliflower rice.

Snack: Edamame beans with sea salt.

Day 3:

Breakfast: Chia seed pudding with coconut milk and sliced kiwi.

Lunch: Falafel wrap with whole wheat pita, lettuce, tomatoes, and tahini sauce.

Dinner: Grilled shrimp skewers with quinoa tabbouleh.

Snack: Celery sticks with peanut butter.

Week 3: Incorporating Different Flavors and Textures

Day 1:

Breakfast: Acai bowl topped with granola, sliced bananas, and shredded coconut.

Lunch: Thai-inspired coconut curry soup with tofu and rice noodles.

Dinner: Stuffed bell peppers with quinoa, black beans, corn, and salsa.

Snack: Rice cakes with almond butter and sliced strawberries.

Day 2:

Breakfast: Mango and pineapple smoothie with coconut water and spinach.

Lunch: Mexican-inspired black bean and corn salad with avocado dressing.

Dinner: Teriyaki salmon with roasted vegetables and brown rice.

Snack: Frozen grapes.

Day 3:

Breakfast: Banana almond butter smoothie with spinach and almond milk.

Lunch: Greek salad with mixed greens, tomatoes, cucumbers, olives, and feta cheese.

Dinner: Baked chicken breast with roasted root vegetables and couscous.

Snack: Cottage cheese with pineapple chunks.

Week 4: Final Week of the Meal Plan with Suggested Modifications

Day 1:

Breakfast: Scrambled eggs with sautéed spinach and whole grain toast.

Lunch: Caprese salad with fresh mozzarella, tomatoes, basil, and balsamic glaze.

Dinner: Beef stir-fry with mixed vegetables and quinoa.

Snack: Trail mix with nuts, seeds, and dried fruit.

Day 2:

Breakfast: Greek yogurt parfait with granola and mixed berries.

Lunch: Spinach and feta stuffed chicken breast with roasted potatoes and green beans.

Dinner: Veggie burger on whole wheat bun with lettuce, tomato, and avocado.

Snack: Veggie sticks with tzatziki dip.

Day 3:

Breakfast: Whole grain waffles with Greek yogurt and sliced peaches.

Lunch: Cobb salad with grilled chicken, hard-boiled eggs, avocado, bacon bits, and blue cheese dressing.

Dinner: Turkey meatballs with marinara sauce and zucchini noodles.

Snack: Almond and coconut energy balls.

By stocking up on nutritious ingredients, you can ensure that you have everything you need to prepare balanced meals and snacks that support blood sugar control and overall health. Here's a comprehensive list of essentials to consider:

1. Fresh Produce:

- ✓ Leafy greens (spinach, kale, Swiss chard)
- ✓ Cruciferous vegetables (broccoli, cauliflower, Brussels sprouts)
- ✓ Colorful vegetables (bell peppers, carrots, tomatoes, and zucchini)
- ✓ Berries (strawberries, blueberries, raspberries)
- ✓ Citrus fruits (lemons, oranges, grapefruits)
- ✓ Avocado
- ✓ Cucumber
- ✓ Onions
- ✓ Garlic
- ✓ Ginger

2. Whole Grains:

- ✓ Quinoa
- ✓ Brown rice
- ✓ Rolled oats
- ✓ Whole wheat pasta
- ✓ Barley

- ✓ Buckwheat
- ✓ Millet

3. Legumes:

- ✓ Lentils (green, brown, red)
- ✓ Chickpeas
- ✓ Black beans
- ✓ Kidney beans
- ✓ Cannellini beans
- ✓ Pinto beans

4. Plant-Based Proteins:

- ✓ Tofu
- ✓ Tempeh
- ✓ Edamame
- ✓ Plant-based protein powders (pea protein, hemp protein)
- ✓ Seitan (wheat gluten)

5. Healthy Fats:

- ✓ Avocado
- ✓ Nuts (almonds, walnuts, pistachios)
- ✓ Seeds (flaxseeds, chia seeds, pumpkin seeds)
- ✓ Nut butters (almond butter, peanut butter)
- ✓ Olive oil

6. Dairy Alternatives:

- ✓ Unsweetened almond milk
- ✓ Unsweetened coconut milk
- ✓ Unsweetened soy milk
- ✓ Plant-based yogurts (coconut, almond, soy)

7. Herbs, Spices, and Condiments:

- ✓ Fresh herbs (parsley, cilantro, basil)
- ✓ Spices (cinnamon, turmeric, cumin, paprika)
- ✓ Low-sodium soy sauce or tamari
- ✓ Vinegars (balsamic, apple cider, rice vinegar)
- ✓ Mustard
- ✓ Tahini
- ✓ Hot sauce

8. Low-Glycemic Sweeteners:

- ✓ Stevia
- ✓ Monk fruit sweetener

- ✓ Erythritol

9. Frozen Foods:

- ✓ Frozen berries
- ✓ Frozen mixed vegetables
- ✓ Frozen edamame
- ✓ Frozen veggie burgers

10. Miscellaneous:

- ✓ Plant-based broth (vegetable broth, mushroom broth)
- ✓ Whole grain bread or wraps
- ✓ Non-dairy cheese alternatives
- ✓ Canned tomatoes
- ✓ Dark chocolate (70% cocoa or higher)

Glossary of Terms

1. Carbohydrates: Macronutrients found in foods like grains, fruits, vegetables, and legumes, which are broken down into glucose and used as the body's primary source of energy.

2. Insulin Resistance: A condition in which cells become less responsive to the effects of insulin, leading to elevated blood sugar levels.

3. Glycemic Index: A ranking system that measures how quickly carbohydrates in foods raise blood sugar levels.

4. Plant-Based Diet: A diet that emphasizes whole, minimally processed plant foods and excludes or minimizes animal products.

5. Fiber: A type of carbohydrate found in plant foods that cannot be digested by the body, aiding in digestion and promoting feelings of fullness.

6. Whole Grains: Grains that contain the entire grain kernel, including the bran, germ, and endosperm, providing essential nutrients and fiber.

7. Phytonutrients: Bioactive compounds found in plant foods that have antioxidant and anti-inflammatory properties, promoting health and reducing the risk of chronic diseases.

8. Omega-3 Fatty Acids: Essential fatty acids found in certain plant foods and fatty fish that are important for brain health, heart health, and reducing inflammation.

9. Saturated Fats: Fats found primarily in animal products and some plant oils, which can raise LDL cholesterol levels and increase the risk of heart disease when consumed in excess.

10. Monounsaturated Fats: Healthy fats found in foods like avocados, nuts, and olive oil, which can improve heart health and reduce inflammation.

11. Polyunsaturated Fats: Healthy fats found in foods like seeds, nuts, and fatty fish, which are important for brain function and reducing inflammation.

12. Cholesterol: A waxy substance found in the blood that can accumulate in the arteries and increase the risk of heart disease when levels are too high.

13. Antioxidants: Compounds found in plant foods that protect cells from damage caused by free radicals, potentially reducing the risk of chronic diseases like cancer and heart disease.

14. Portion Control: The practice of eating appropriate serving sizes to manage calorie intake and promote weight loss or weight maintenance.

15. Meal Planning: The process of organizing and preparing meals in advance, often to support health goals like weight loss, blood sugar control, or balanced nutrition.

16. Blood Glucose Monitoring: The regular testing of blood sugar levels to track how food, physical activity, medication, and other factors affect blood sugar control.

17. Nutrient Density: A measure of the nutrients provided by a food relative to its calorie content, with nutrient-dense foods providing more nutrients per calorie.

18. Hydration: The process of maintaining adequate fluid balance in the body by consuming enough water and other fluids.

19. Superfoods: Nutrient-rich foods that are particularly beneficial for health due to their high levels of vitamins, minerals, antioxidants, or other bioactive compounds.

20. Diabetes Management: The ongoing process of monitoring blood sugar levels, making lifestyle changes, and taking medications as needed to control diabetes and reduce the risk of complications.

Thank You

Thank you for purchasing and reading this book! Your commitment to improving your health with a plant-based approach to managing type 2 diabetes is commendable. I hope the information, recipes, and resources provided empower you on your journey towards better health and well-being. Here's to embracing delicious, nourishing meals and making positive changes for a vibrant life ahead.

Milton Keynes UK
Ingram Content Group UK Ltd.
UKHW021741120824
1235UKWH00075B/2086